HANGING

BY A

GOD THREAD

BY: KELLY ANN DEGEARE

Dedication

I dedicate this book to our children Harrison and Sarah, whom we have been blessed to have God entrust to us.

Harrison, we are soo proud of the faith and courage you have shown ever since the news of your heart "challenges". We are excited to see the man of God you are growing up to be, and pray you will always *seek God first* and trust your life to Him.

I also want to dedicate this story of faith to my friend and sister in Christ, Alicia Moffitt. For right now, she is walking 'her' journey of faith while the family waits upon the Lord for the health of their daughter, Noelle, age 2. If you are reading this, I ask that you please pray for the Moffitt family and sweet little Noelle who has to go weekly to Loma Linda for treatments.

> "We walk by faith, not by sight." (II Corinthians 5:7)

I love you my sister, Alicia, and God WILL walk you through this and make GOOD from all things!

Anyone else reading this who may also be struggling, I pray that somehow this book will encourage YOU to know God is with you, right by your side, and He shall never leave or forsake you!

> "And the Lord, He is the One who goes before you. He will be with you, He will NOT leave you nor forsake you, do not fear nor be dismayed." (Deuteronomy 31:8)

Acknowledgments

I would like to thank the following people for their support and encouragement:

My loving and patient husband, David

My Mom, for her selfless love and sacrifices

Pastor Jason Duff, for GROUNDING me in the Word

Sean Wyman, for encouragement

Adam Flores, for believing in me

Cherie Aimee, for never letting me have excuses!!!

Belinda Rainwater, my editor and friend

Desiree Lee for *Authors in Business* group and her support

My son, Harrison, for his tech support

My daughter, Sarah, for helping with artwork

Lynn Wyman, for her graphic talent

Table of Contents

Foreword

Hanging by a God Thread

One of the five major sacrifices outlined in the book of Leviticus that the priests would offer on behalf of themselves and the people of God was the burnt sacrifice. What made this sacrifice unique was the fact that unlike other sacrifices where part of the animal was saved and shared as food and fellowship between the offeror and the priests, the burnt sacrifice was totally consumed on the alter. The people would offer this sacrifice to say to the Lord, 'This is what I want my life to be, totally surrendered to You, totally consumed by You, God.' Kelly DeGeare's story "Hanging by a God Thread", is an account of just such a life – a life that desires to be totally consumed by the Lord. Her story will both encourage you _and_ challenge you to have your life laid down before the Lord – not just as a burnt sacrifice totally consumed by the Lord – but a living sacrifice as well.

Pastor Jason Duff
The Garden Fellowship
January 18th, 2017

CHAPTER 1

"Are You Sure?"

It was 2am.

Although I'm usually a deep sleeper, my "momma mode" kicked in and I sprang to my feet when I heard my son call my name. "Mom..." he said. I ran into his room to see what was wrong. My seven-year-old Harrison was telling me that his chest hurt. I really am not one to immediately think the worst, so I just said, "It's probably just heartburn or indigestion." And, I calmly told him to go back to sleep after I rubbed his back for a while.

Well, just a couple nights later, about 2am, my little boy yelled for me again. It was for the exact same thing. My son told me again that his chest was hurting.

The next day was a Friday and I had to ask, "Why it is that you always need to call the doctor on the weekends?"

We had really good insurance at the time and since my birthday was just the next week, I thought, *Let's go for a special mother/son lunch, and take off for the day to go see the heart doctor.* We could go do lunch and get the tests done – just to make sure. The doctor wouldn't find anything wrong, right?

I think back now and still wonder, *I didn't even have my husband go with me.* I was sure it was simple and actually was not prepared for what the doctor was about to tell me. So, after all the testing, the EKGs, echocardiograms, and ultrasounds, the heart doctor came into the waiting room where we were sitting. Isn't it strange how just by a "look" in someone's eyes, you can tell something is wrong?

Well, as the doctor walked in, I knew whatever it was he was going to tell me right then, I maybe should have our son wait in the other room.

This will give you an understanding of which decade it was, as I asked our son, Harrison, to go in the other room and play his DS. As he did just that, I swear the next 5 minutes seemed like one of those out-of-body experiences as the doctor began to speak.

"Well, Mrs. DeGeare, let me get a piece of paper so I can explain what is going on." Of course, in my head I am saying, *What is he going to show me? How difficult can heartburn or indigestion be?* since I was still convinced that is what the problem was.

"You see, normally we all have three valves in our heart. Your son has only two valves. We call this a "bicuspid" aorta type of heart."

I'm sure the doctor must have seen my disbelief as he stopped, but then continued as my mouth opened wide and the tears started rolling down my cheeks. I am certain I made him feel uneasy.

Honestly, after that first thing he said, I really felt like I was not even in my body. Instead, I was looking down on him as his voice just became a "numb" sound, kind of like the one in Charlie Brown when the teacher speaks.

As he handed me the piece of white, thin paper that he had drawn on with his black pen, my one big question and all I could ask was, "Are you sure? Are you _sure_ you have the right charts? Maybe this is someone else's?" I remember like it was yesterday. "No, ma'am. I'm sorry."

"So, what does this mean?" I asked, trying to muster up enough courage and strength.

"Well," the heart doctor said, "he definitely won't be able to play sports. We have to monitor his heart every three months to see how it is doing. We want to try to not over-exert the heart muscle, so no weight lifting, and that sort of thing."

I think that was all I could take, and all I could swallow really, along with the other information of our son actually "missing" a valve in his heart. *Was this for real?*

You see, I had the most perfect pregnancy. I remember like it was just yesterday. I never ate tuna, which is my favorite, because they said the mercury was bad for the baby. I ate wheat germ like it was going out of style. I never had lunch meat because of the nitrates. I never ate shrimp as they said it was a "bottom dweller" and was not safe. I kept phenylalanine out of my diet, and I would never even dream of having a hot dog! In fact, once Harrison was born, that was all I wanted my girlfriend to bring me to the hospital to eat, was a Costco hot dog! Thank you, Lisa Walker!!!

So, my point is, nobody could figure out from where this "heart issue" could have even developed. And better yet, how... why... no one even detected it when he was first born?

Well, actually, I am very grateful they did not as they probably would have told me to operate and put a pig valve in, or something crazy like that! So, I am glad God protected us there to totally rely on Him instead.

CHAPTER 2

"What Did They Say, Mom?"

Walking out to the car with my son, I was sure not ready for the drive home, nor what my son was about to ask me.

Harrison vaulted into the back seat as any normal seven-year-old would do, sat in his car seat, and as we drove away, he looked at me in the rear-view mirror and asked in his sweet voice, "What did they say, Mom?"

So many things ran through my head at that moment. I wanted to make sure to instill courage and hope in our son – definitely not fear – and let him know how much God loved him. ...that He has a plan for his life. Remember, he was only 7 at the time. I knew that whatever I was about to say would stay with him for the rest of his life...

"Well, buddy. You know how smart you are in spelling and math? Well, God has a special plan for your life. You have a unique heart. You know how some guys do weight lifting? And go to the gym? Well, God made _you_ in a way that your body is not supposed to do that."

I will never forget his sweet little eyes as he listened to me, looking at me from the rear-view mirror in the car, as we drove home.

He said, "You know, Mommy, those guys aren't really that smart anyway!"

Now, that turned the tears that I was holding back into a chuckle, which was a good thing.

Harrison always was a smart boy, especially for his age. But, how do you tell a seven-year-old boy not to be "too physical"?

I knew many challenges would lie ahead for us, and really wondered, along with losing our house, and going through bankruptcy, how was I even going to handle it all?

CHAPTER 3

Explaining to Daddy

I have to say I usually do take care of all the kids' stuff, but this is ONE time I wish I had taken daddy with us.

My husband works very hard and is usually gone during the day, so I had to wait until he got home to tell him. Of course, he rushed home that day to find out what the doctor had said.

Standing alone, just the two of us in the bedroom, he asked, "So what does this mean? We need to go back to the doctor each year to check on his heart?"

As I held out my hand and pointed to the space between us, I said, "No, honey, we are right here, right where Jesus wants us to be, relying on him _every_ second. …the doctor said every 3 months for life!"

He was silent for a moment, and I continued, trying to be as gentle and positive as I could. The doctor also said, 'Until we know more, your son should not play any sports, and definitely no weightlifting or isometric exercises.'

Being a man and a lover of sports, I can only imagine what went through his head, being told that his son could never play sports.

I have to tell you, since we had recently bankrupted and we were in the process of losing our home, this was about the LAST thing we needed to hear, or could have ever imagined having to deal with.

All that kept running through my head was *Lord, is this really happening to us?* I had had such a great and healthy pregnancy. How could this even happen? I don't recall ever being mad at God, that was just never my go-to place. But, I still could not figure out why ... *WHY* all of this was happening, and HOW, ***HOW*** was I ever going to get through it?!?!

My husband took all this in and went off to be alone – I guess to pray and think of what was next.

> "Your word is a lamp unto my feet, and a light unto my path." (Psalms 119:105)

CHAPTER 4

Letting It All Sink In

During this time, it sure did not help that we were also bankrupting and losing our home at Stonegate Homes, in Bermuda Dunes, California. I literally felt like Job, in the middle of the desert, wandering for 40 years!!! And, just everything crumbling around me, left and right...

You know what did help? We just happened to be at the Garden Fellowship Church, and had just started attending there six months before. We were in Hebrews and the halls of faith, and learning about Abraham, Isaac, Moses, and more!!!!

Boy! What the pastor was talking about with Abraham, Isaac, Moses, and Jacob, and the unshakeable faith that they had. I tell you what! I was there soaking it ALL in and hanging on e-v-e-r-y l-a-s-t word he was speaking. The faith that each of these men had and how incredible and strong it was!!!

As I sit here right now, writing this, and watching my son who is now 14, playing his favorite sport – basketball – I am in awe of Our Lord, Our Healer, Our Almighty God, for the miracle of my son even being able to play ball!

During this "walk in the desert", one huge, epic moment was realizing this... "God is not pleased without Faith!" Oh, I get it now!!! I am telling you, my whole world came "full circle" with this verse. THIS is now my life verse, as it all made sense to me somehow, and it will forever be on my heart and lips!!!

> "For God is not pleased without faith, and all those that come to Him must believe that He is, and He is a rewarder of those that diligently seek Him." (Hebrews 11:6)

So, with the bankruptcy, our four-year-old Sarah battling pneumonia at the time, losing our home, getting robbed, and moving back to our humble house in La Quinta, _and_ finding out this news of our son's heart missing a valve, it ALL made sense to me now...THIS is what pleases our Lord...our FAITH!!!!!!!

I learned how God does not "cause things" but He can "allow" them, as we are living in a sinful world. This is why there is pain, suffering, and brokenness in the first place.

It is through these trials, that He draws near to us, and we draw near to Him, and this is what I was learning firsthand.

CHAPTER 5

On My Knees

One thing I was grateful for was that if I just rolled over out of bed, the floor was not too far for me to go. This was good for me, as when I would FALL out of bed, I would be right where I needed to be…on my knees!!!

My life at that time, feeling like the floor was being pulled out from under me, it was pretty much an easy 'go-to' for me to surrender everything to Jesus. I would start each day basically saying to God, "Okay, God. Here is my life. I **_cannot_** handle all these things happening to me, so I give it all to You! I throw it at Your feet and may whatever happens bring You glory somehow."

Was it easy? No!!!

But, was it necessary? Yes!!!

Was it worth it? A huge YES and AMEN!!!!!

One thing I think that really rolled around in my head at that time was the difference between was God "causing" things that were bad, or was God "allowing" these things to happen…?

So many people who are not Believers often ask that question, 'Why would a loving God allow bad things to happen to good people?'

Honestly, one day, when I get to heaven, that is one thing I cannot wait to ask, "Did Harrison have this heart condition when he was born, or was it something the enemy was allowed to make happen? Or was it You, God? Showing the enemy the faith that I had, that even with ALL the bad things going on, that I would STILL give You all the honor and glory?!" It will be a good question.

This was really a big deal for me, and I think also, a big deal for many others, too. Just that question alone, *Does God "cause" things? Or does He "allow" things for us to grow and become more reliant on Him?*

You see, what needs to be explained here, for those reading who may not be Believers or Christian, is this:

Our God is a loving God, caring, merciful and so full of grace. He loves us so much, but sadly this world is broken, and already sinful from back in the garden with Adam and Eve. It was broken when Eve gave in to temptation in the garden. From then forward, sin came into existence.

So, because sin is present, there will be pain, there will be sorrow, there will be death and destruction. That is why the Lord, who is the only Perfect One, had to take our sin upon Him on the cross.

The wonderful thing is that we can boldly come to Him and firmly rely on His words in His book, The Bible. He has His promises and instructions there for us, for our daily life. For His promises, I am very grateful.

> "For He made Him who knew no sin to be sin for us, that we might become the righteousness of God in Him. (II Corinthians 5:21)

CHAPTER 6

So, What's Next?

At the time, when my husband David and I got the news of our son's heart concerns (I never once have allowed it to be called a "heart disease") we were attending Jordan Outreach Ministry School in Coachella. As I look back now, I am in awe of how God had us right where He knew we needed to be.

If you are reading this book and have never been to nor heard of Jordan Ministries, I implore you to do so. God is doing a mighty work out there, sharing the hope and love of Jesus with all His precious children in the East Valley. They have a kids' club and they host many wonderful events. They are also involved in feeding and blessing many throughout the year.

Rob Manley is involved with the kids' club and serves with Pastor Joe Jordan, who started this ministry years ago. (See the back cover for information on this wonderful ministry and an opportunity to serve, pray, or donate). Rob even goes to pick up the kids in the church bus for those who cannot get there!

So, here we were with the news that our son is missing a valve in his heart. Money was an issue. We were going through bankruptcy, losing our home, and we got robbed in the middle of the day while moving. To top it off, our daughter, Sarah, age 3 (at that time), had pneumonia and had to get a shot each day for a week straight. (And believe me, that was no easy task!)

We have a joke at our house. One day, should she marry a doctor, she won't even take his lunch to him. This is how much she despises going to the doctor. I was literally taking her every day, kicking and screaming, for these shots. It was a struggle I won't soon forget. With everything else going on, it broke my heart even more to see her suffer.

Each day, as I took my two kids to school at Jordan Outreach, there was this 35-foot white metal cross that gave me a sweet visual of what exactly I needed to be doing.

So, every day at their school, I literally threw _everything_ at the foot of that cross. Surrender is a great thing. And actually, I feel the answer to everything when it comes to walking with Jesus.

I just have to say, at this particular part of the book, there are a few people I am humbled and blessed that God had placed in our lives during this time right after we found out the news about Harrison's heart. Thank you Pastor Joe

Jordan, Nannette Battles, Denise Hernandez, Shana Howard, and Terry Hamilton. Each played a crucial role in our life, not only in our prayer group, but individually in their own way. I am extremely thankful and forever grateful to and for each one.

I will never forget how Nannette Battles and Denise Hernandez were there when we prayed in agreement for a healing for Harrison, and put oil on him. I am so thankful for these Sisters in Christ for believing with me in his miracle.

> "Therefore, I say unto you, whatever things you ask when you pray, believe that you receive them and you will have them." (Mark 11:24) (And these are in the red letters when Jesus is speaking.)

CHAPTER 7

The Homeschool Answer to Prayer

Now, although Jordan Outreach School was a HUGE blessing in our life at that time, we really didn't know enough about the physical challenges our son, Harrison, then 7, would have. (That is pretty special – this chapter happens to be 7 and it was 7 years ago *today* that this whole journey started... More on the special number 7 another time).

We did not fully know the challenges that lay ahead of us. We did not know if Harrison would pass out when he ran on the playground, or what exactly his limitations were. You see, as previously mentioned, we were told by his pediatrician, Dr. Hashmi in Palm Springs, who has been amazing this whole journey, that Harrison at the onset of the findings, should not play sports. Each person is different, and we needed to see how he "progressed", in time.

For the moment, at that time, I had begun to pray for wisdom and for God to direct us for what was next.

> "But as for me, I would seek God, and to God I would commit my cause." (John 5:8)

Harrison was 7 at that time, and being a boy it was hard to drop him off at school and tell him what he could and could not do physically. It was at that time my husband David and I really prayed about homeschooling. Harrison was in the third grade, and our daughter Sarah was in kindergarten.

Being a stay-at-home mom and working independently as a wellness consultant, as well as an interior design consultant, we could see how we could make this work. David and I felt God's peace for this homeschooling "season" for us.

Harrison was actually playing soccer at the time, so David and I decided to coach the team. We did this so that we could choose the drills and exercises to make sure they were not isometric and would not compromise his heart condition. I often thought I would always look at our son differently when he played.

It is interesting to discuss all of this now as "a-matter-of-fact" and with "ease", seven years later. It has been the struggle and the journey of these seven years that was necessary to understand God's perfect timing and His perfect will and "walk in that peace".

At the time all this was happening, what to do? What did this mean? Or how do we handle this? I was literally being "carried" by the Lord! That is the best way I can describe it.

It seems simple now, having come this far seven years down the road – or in the desert, as I would say…like Job did for forty years. That is why the cover of this book has a thin, small "thread" that I was hanging from, and how it is now a big, thick, beefy "rope". This represents my walk with the Lord and how it has transformed into this strong rope, unable to be broken.

> "My brethren, count it all joy when you fall into diverse temptation, knowing this that the trying of your faith worketh patience." (James 1:2-3)

I cannot leave chapter 7, without sharing the "visual" that God gave me during this "trial".

I know this is crazy, and may seem extreme, but this **IS** what God gave me to fully understand "surrender" and what that looks like.

I have to share, as I really am a numbers person, and the Lord often speaks and confirms to me using numbers. One huge reason 7 is my number – and I could literally write a whole book about that number – is the many "confirmations" the Lord has given me through that number 7.

Okay, so back to the most important lesson I think I have learned thus far ... and that is about complete surrender!!!!

What I think is so super cool is that when our amazing Pastor Jason Duff, was going through Genesis with us, little did I know God had another "number" gift for me.

You see, the story and "visual" God gave me to truly embrace the word "surrender", was that story of Abraham and Isaac.

> "Now it came to pass after these things that God tested Abraham, and said to him, 'Abraham!' and he said, 'Here I am.' Then He said, 'Take now your only son, Isaac, whom you love, and go to the land of Moriah, and offer him there as a burnt offering on one of the mountains of which I shall tell you.'" (Genesis 22:1-2)

You see, God had not really _intended_ for Abraham to offer his son up for a sacrifice, and once God saw and knew that the faith of Abraham was enough, He had him stop. God provided the ram for the Living Sacrifice, and did not need him to go further, once He saw his "Faith".

To me, in my mind, I gave the Lord my son. He was not mine in the first place. He was born to me as a gift, but truly belonged to the Lord. The news of his heart, along with losing our home and all the other things we were dealing with – it was just more than I could handle _on my own_.

In my mind and in my heart, I did just that. I left my son at the Lord's feet for **HIM** to take care of, and to do His will, fully. I just, completely and humbly, surrendered to our Lord Jesus Christ.

It was in that special, profound moment, that a peace rushed over me unlike anything I have ever experienced in my life.

> "I will both lie down in peace, and sleep, for You alone, oh Lord, make me dwell in safety." (Psalm 4:8)

To me, by surrendering our son to God, He has rewarded us in so many ways. In my mind and heart, He has given our son back to us by blessing us with the miracle of Harrison being able to play his beloved sport – basketball.

You see, another very cool gift from the Lord, is the picture He gave to me in my heart is the same story as in Genesis 22. The 22nd also happens to be the day that our son was born. Only our God would know of such a thing long before Harrison was even born.

Indeed!!!!!!!! It is more than a special gift, but yet another true Miracle of FAITH!!!!

I will always treasure the fact that the story of Abraham and Isaac that God put upon my heart is in Genesis 22, as this just confirms to me that I was being obedient and that is what the Lord wanted me to do.

"But you, when you pray, go into your room, and when you have shut your door, pray to your Father who is in the secret place, and your Father who sees in secret will reward you openly." (Matthew 6:6)

CHAPTER 8

We Will See You In 6 Months…

Up until now, we were told we would need to get Harrison checked every 3 months, for life. This would include an EKG, echocardiogram, ultrasound, and other tests to make sure there were no changes in his heart.

God had us right where He wanted us, on our knees, surrendering daily to Him and totally relying on Him for all things.

I am so grateful to the Lord for being so real, so present, and so close during this period of time. It is so true how each circumstance, trial, and season brings us that much closer to the Father. (This is also why I chose to use the red rope on the front cover which means "Tikvah" in Hebrew and represents the "hope" that we have in Jesus. When you look at the back cover of this book, you can see how intricate, healthy, woven, and strong it is. This represents my faith now and how abundant it is. Not only in size, but in strength!

I can remember like it was yesterday. Our son was about eight now, and going to Dr. Hashmi for our regular check-up. It is funny how I said "our" instead of "his" checkup. I guess, as a mom, you truly take on all things that our children go through, as I am sure any mom out there can relate.

Anyway, we went through the EKG and all the testing. Dr. Hashmi came back to consult with us, and I will never forget his words. "Okay, well, since things are looking so great and there have been no changes, we can see you guys back in 6 months." Wow! Really? Wait! *What*?

Are you *sure*??

I was overwhelmed again with this news, and God's grace for covering us, and more answers to prayer!
Dr. Hashmi said, "Whatever it is you are doing, keep doing it!"

I had to hesitate when I said, "Absolutely nothing, just praying! That is all we are doing, PRAYING!!!!!! And having faith in Jesus for healing!" Dr. Hashmi said, "This is great news. Keep it up!"

I remember leaving the doctor's office and just thanking the Lord so much for this answer to prayer. Also though, saying at the same time "Lord, please do not go anywhere!

You have not left me, right? Please stay by my side as You have been, and do not leave me alone!"

I knew the Lord had not left me, but it was just such a weird feeling getting this news to **NOT** come back for six months. I just had to pray to God to say "Please, don't go away from me, because I _**need**_ Your closeness." Even driving away from the doctor's office, I cried out to him repeatedly, "God, don't leave me now!"

Believe me, I never, not even for a single day, have taken for granted the little things. Getting this news was such a big blessing!

> You are my God, and I will praise you, you are my God, I will exalt you!" (Psalms 118:28)

CHAPTER 9

The Medical Bracelet

"And they overcame by the blood of the Lamb and the Word of their testimony!" (Revelation 12:10)

The only thing that Harrison was told he needed to do was wear this silver medical bracelet that has his name, phone number, and his heart condition written on it in case of an emergency. If he was ever in an accident, he is required to have antibiotics prior to surgery, so that his blood does not get contaminated.

Well, this has not been an easy thing to do, to make him wear this bracelet, for some reason. I do not know if it's because he truly does not like to wear jewelry, or because he did not like anyone asking about it, or feeling like he was different, or had a "problem".

Here is how I explained it.

"Harrison, sometimes things happen to us, so that we can give God glory for what He has done in and through us in different situations."

I do believe he now "gets" this, and actually, one night after a Junior High group, he came home and told me, "Mom, tonight I shared my testimony about my heart and how God has healed me." His pastor, Taylor Corum, was there, which made it extra special.

You can only imagine how incredibly blessed and proud I was when I heard this, and still am every day.

I also have used this opportunity to share with our son how God does not "cause" bad things to happen, but that we are already born in a fallen and sinful world, and that bad things do happen. I explained to Harrison about God's promises in His word, that He will make good from it, and if it is His will, we will be able to see that. I continued to share that sometimes we are not able to see right away the reasons why some things happen, but that we need faith and have to trust in God.

> "For I know the plans I have for you says the Lord, thoughts of peace and not of evil, to give you hope for the future." (Jeremiah 29:11)

CHAPTER 10

FAITH: Day by Day…

I honestly don't think a day goes by that I do not think about or am grateful for, pray about or give to God the glory for all that He has done in our son, Harrison. Also, during this time of personal battle, I am very grateful for the courage God gave me through it all.

Just this past year, 2016, our wonderful pastor and friend, Jason Duff, along with a few church elders and friends, prayed with my husband, David and I, along with our son at church.

We had been told by the doctor that we needed to really watch and see that there continue to be no changes in Harrison's heart, or we would need to look at taking medication, or consider other alternatives.

We all prayed in agreement for God's healing and laid hands upon Harrison that there would be no change at his next appointment.

I remember again _totally_ trusting in God for His will and surrendering our son, Harrison, to Him.

The appointment was about one month after this prayer gathering, so each day after that was all about trusting and waiting upon the Lord. That is truly the song and mantra of my life, 'My strength will rise as we wait upon the Lord, we will wait upon the Lord...' for this is what He wants us to do.

The most important thing I learned during this season, is that it is _Faith_ that pleases God, and that we truly..._truly_...t-r-u-l-y need to wait upon the Lord as that is where He wants us to be all the time.

> "Therefore, I will look to the Lord, I will wait for the God of my salvation, my God will hear me!" (Micah 7:7) (I JUST LOVE that THIS verse is 7– IT IS His perfect number of completion!!!)

During this time of waiting, and truly relying on God in all areas of our life, beauty happens. This is where Jesus deepens the bond of our faith, and we grow closer to the Father and He strengthens us in that waiting period.

At this last visit at Dr. Hashmi's office he told us this, "Even though there is no change now, I just want you to be prepared in the future if we ever need to start medication – to be open to that if changes happen."

I just recalled the last time we barely tried medication for a week. Harrison got a bad stomach ache and was very nauseous. It was then that I prayed and asked for wisdom and felt God saying to rely on Him, and have faith yet again. In Him all things are possible, for there is nothing too big for our God.

It is funny. Once you go through so much loss, hardship, hurt, and adversity, each trial that comes along seems to get easier. Once we learn to "surrender" to our Heavenly Father, who loves us so much, there is **<u>nothing</u>** that can replace that feeling.

The more you truly seek Jesus, get on your knees, read His Living Word, and humble yourself before Him, He will meet you in that place and speak to your heart in so many ways.

> "If any of you lack wisdom, let him ask of God, that giveth to all men liberally, and without reproach, and it shall be given to him." (James 1:5)

I am so grateful to God for walking us through this journey and for speaking to my heart in a real and practical way.

I remember one time at our church, the Garden Fellowship, when we were actually outside at a real garden at a nursery, and the pastor at that time had us in the book of Hebrews.

He asked us all to close our eyes, and hold out our hands, and he asked us this question...

'Is there any trial, any loss, any tragedy, any painful season that you would trade for your walk with Jesus?'

As I tried to hold back the tears as they trickled down my cheek, I said to my God, "No, not one. Not even one. Not even my son's heart would I trade for Thee."

It was that day and moving forward, I knew my loving Father in Heaven would never leave me or forsake me, that He is my God and He is mighty to save! And yes! THAT is another song, *Mighty to Save*, that I sing LOUDLY and boldly while giving Him Glory for all that He HAS done and ALL He is going to do in not only my life, but in *yours* as well.

I am now excited, humbled, and blessed to be an Ambassador for Jesus!!!!

I feel confident in stepping into my calling, to stand firm on the gifts He has given me, and profess my faith to further His kingdom.

I pray for you to make this decision to accept Jesus into your life, to live a life free from guilt, free from hurt, free from pain. For Jesus is our pain taker and our chain breaker!!!!! I hope that you will make this decision if you have not already, so that one day when you get to Heaven , our Lord can say, "Well done good and faithful servant, enter in!"

AMEN

"If you confess with your mouth the Lord Jesus and believe in your heart that God has raised him from the dead, you will be saved." (Romans 10:9)

Connecting with the Author

Please connect with me at humblehandyman@aol.com
The community: CHOOSE TO CHANGE
Instagram @kellydegeare or
FaceBook with messenger

I would love to connect.

God's Blessings to you always!!!!!

A Special Thank You and an Opportunity to Give Back

Joe Jordan and Jordan Outreach Ministries
P.O. Box 818
Thermal, California, 92274
(760) 398-3352

Please pray for and if so led, help support this ministry
which touches so many lives and helps so many children in
need.

Also, if you wish to support another ministry, God is doing
BIG things through missions and more:

www.thegardenfellowship.com
Pastor Jason Duff
(760) 360-0686

Thank you for your prayers and support!!! God Bless His
kingdom and its servants!!!

Made in the USA
Middletown, DE
10 February 2017